MUSIC CLASSIFICATION

MUSIC CLASSIFICATION

Schedule for Colon Classification

Dr. Mohammed Haroon
M.A., M.Lib. Inf. Sc., Ph.D
(Deputy Librarian)
Delhi University Library System
University of Delhi

KANISHKA PUBLISHERS, DISTRIBUTORS
NEW DELHI-110 002

KANISHKA PUBLISHERS, DISTRIBUTORS
4697/5-21 A, Ansari Road, Daryaganj
New Delhi-110 002
Phones : 2327 0497, 2328 8285
Fax : 011-2328 8285
E-mail: kanishka_publishing@yahoo.co.in

First Published 2010

ISBN 978-81-8457-108-7

PRINTED IN INDIA

Published by Madan Sachdeva for Kanishka Publishers, Distributors, 4697/5-21A, Ansari Road, Daryaganj, New Delhi-110 002, Typeset by Sunshine Graphics, Delhi, and Printed at Rajdhani Printers, Delhi.

As my humble homage

This book is

DEDICATED TO

(Late) Shri SHER SINGH
Ex Deputy Librarian,
Delhi University Library System
University of Delhi

For his inspiration, encouragement and guidance
I am deeply obliged to him.

Preface

Indian music is one of the oldest music systems of the world. From time to time, the scholars have contributed to the spiral of music knowledge that has descended upon us in the form of oral traditions, manuscripts and published works in many languages. In the late nineteenth century, the Britishers started education at university and college levels. But prior to it, some musicians had established music teaching institutions as early as 1871. After independence, central and state governments made all efforts to provide education to all and music got its due share. Today more than a hundred Indian universities provide music education at all levels. The recorded music registered its advent in 1902 when T W Gainberg came to India and recorded the native talent on 'wax process'. This was a welcome experience for Indian music.

Indian music is very rich in its traditions with glorious past and promising future. Yet there are many dark lines in silvery clouds. Preservation and maintenance of music materials is poor. Manuscripts are scattered with no proper care and documentation. Earlier British and Indian gramophone companies were commercial firms unconcerned with preservation of Indian musical heritage. The British Government also failed towards its duty of establishing some kind of music library, archives or academy. The early recorded music from India almost has been lost and whatever remains is in private custody with a high risk of being lost.

Today more than a hundred Indian universities offer research courses in music and produce large number of

Ph.D's each year. Most of such universities do not have separate music libraries. Here the music collection is part of central library. In such libraries, the audio collection is placed in a corner. The music books are classified by general schemes of classification *e.g.* DDC or CC that are unsuitable and insufficient for the vast literature of this subject that has manifested itself into many branches. Many indices, guides and catalogues were scanned to locate material related with music libraries, archives and collections. The result showed that only two articles have appeared in the Journal Sangeet Natak. Practically there is no literature on music libraries in India.

I am looking after the Library, Faculty of Music & Fine Arts, University of Delhi since 1986. For classifying books on Indian music, first DDC 18 was used but the work was abandoned. Later CC6 was used for the same job that met the same fate.

For the last twenty years, I have been working for designing the depth schedules for Indian music. The progress has been slow as these have been evolved step by step. Once draft for these schedules was ready, these were tested by classifying the books. So many shortcomings were noticed and the changes were made. I hope that my labour will be successful and the work shall be helpful to the libraries in their efforts for organization of their music collections. These schedules have been drafted in the frame of CC6. All the schedules of CC6 shall be used with it. Practically, this is only extension and expansion of the main classes MNR and NR.

Dr. S Majumdar as the Head of the Delhi University Library System, University of Delhi has always been the source of inspiration, guidance and encouragement to his colleagues. I am obliged to him. I am thankful to Prof. Anjali Mittal, Dean Faculty of Music & Fine Arts, for providing peaceful academic environment in the library. The Faculty library was my laboratory where I conceived, designed and tested the drafted schedules. I owe my sincere gratitude to staff members – Mr. M P Mishra, Mrs. Anju Bisht, Mr. Maha Singh, Mr. Dhan Raj and Mrs. Chitra for their full cooperation.

Last but not the least my special thanks to my wife Shama, children Wasi and Tooba for their encouragement to carry on my work. My grand children Maham, Fahad and Aamna should be appreciated for allowing their *nanaji* to complete his home assignments.

Dr. Mohammed Haroon

Foreword

During my long innings of librarianship in various top libraries, I have confronted with difficulties faced by library classifiers. It is true that foreign library classification schemes *e.g.* Library of Congress (LC) or Dewey Decimal Classification (DDC) have little information for classifying literature related with Indian religions, culture and performing arts including music. Dr. Ranganathan's Colon Classification (CC) sixth edition and the new seventh edition have scanty provisions for Indian classical music and dance. In India many universities and other music education institutions are fully dedicated to the performing arts. These institutions have large size libraries. They are experiencing difficulties in classifying their music collections. Practically literature for music librarianship is not available.

Dr. Mohammed Haroon is a well known author with half a dozen books and more than a dozen articles on the subjects/topics that are more or less untouched by others. This small book is a valuable result of his years' labour. I am pleased to know that he has tested these schedules by classifying the music collection of his library. In the last he has provided classified index of the music books and articles. This section provides ready made class numbers and shall be much useful to the classifiers. This index convinces the readers about shelf arrangement of the music collections. They shall be able to browse all the books on vocal music under NR at one place followed by writings on music instruments under NRV. The folk music is an emerging field and printed material is coming out in large quantity.

Documents related with folk music shall be classified in the class number NRY.

A depth schedule for Indian music was drastically needed and Dr. Haroon has successfully accomplished the job. I hope the library fraternity shall be benefited by this book.

I congratulate him for his efforts and wish him success in life.

Dr. S. Majumdar
University Librarian
Delhi University Library System

Contents

1

Music Activities in India: A Survey

Indian civilization is one of the oldest civilizations of the world. So our religious, social and music systems are very old. During Vedic period (5000-4000 B.C.) the knowledge was imparted to students orally. The Vedas were composed in hymns and the students learnt these by heart. These Vedas and Puranas may be considered genesis of music activities. In the beginning these hymns were simple chanting. Gradually singing improved with emphasis on syllables, words and modulation of voice. Two great Indian epics—The Ramayana and the Mahabharata are connected with events that took place between 1000 and 700 B.C. Both of these have references to music and music instruments.

Bharata's Natya Sastra (300 B.C.) is perhaps the oldest and detailed presentation of music theory where all aspects of music have been described. Brahdesi of Matang (900 A.D.) is another important work that mentions ragas system. Dattilam-an Indian ancient work of about 700 A.D. is considered the earliest music dictionary. In the thirteenth century an authoritative work on music namely Sangita Ratnakara was authored by Sarangdeva. This work deals with vocal and instrumental music.

Medieval Period

By the twelve century Muslims came to India from Afghanistan and Iran. They had their own music system.

Under the influence of Persian and Arabic music, the Indian music underwent many favourable changes. Many music books were written in Persian language. Amir Khusro's writings have much music materials. Some other music books in Persian language are Ghunyat-ul-Munya (1374-75 A.D.) and Lehjat-e-Sikandar Shahi (1580-1627 A.D.). In addition to these, there are many books in Persian having references to Indian music. After 1857 when Urdu replaced Persian, music books were written and published in Urdu language.

British Period

The British Government was established in 1857. They introduced European political, social and educational institutions. The European indologists highlightened Indian golden heritage. They translated into English many books from Sanskrit, Persian and other vernacular languages. The foreign authors *e.g.* Captain Williard (1793), William Jones (1793), E Clements (1913) and A H Fox Strangways (1914) wrote books on Indian music. These books deal mainly with history and theory of Indian music.

Archives

Man is a social animal and preservation is a human instinct. Our social customs, caste, creeds and religious beliefs have come to us through the habit of preservation. Our music has come to us orally from ancient period and may be termed as oral archives.

Cushioned in the hoary antiquity of several millennia, the cultural heritage of India descends down to us through the manuscripts that constitute one of the several sources of very valuable information for the social, cultural and literary history of India.[1] No one knows the manuscript wealth of India. To preserve this wealth for the next generation Indira Gandhi National Centre for the Arts (New Delhi) has been assigned the job for digitalizing the manuscript wealth from all over India.

Formal Music Education

In India music education at university and college levels started late. But in the nineteenth century some persons had established music teaching institutions at many places. The first such school for music was established in 1871 by Shri Khetra Mohan Goswami. In 1874 Pandit Bhaskar Rao Bakhle started his school namely 'Bharat Gayan Samaj' in Pune (Maharashtra). In 1886 Shrimat Sayaji Rao Gaikward established another school at Baroda (now Vedora) that later on became Baroda State Music School. In early 20th century two stewart of Indian music – Pandit Paluskar and Pandit Bhatkhande established many music schools at different places of undivided India.

After independence, the central and state governments made all efforts to provide education to more and more people. New universities were established all over India. Today more than one hundred universities provide music education at graduate, post graduate levels with research facilities. It may be mentioned here that in India first Ph.D degrees were awarded in 1950 to two research scholars by Madras and Saugar Universities and after a gap of ten years in 1960 one Ph.D was awarded by Banaras Hindu University and two Ph.D's were given by Kerala University. Now University Grants Commission has made research degree as a pre-condition to promotion and so research activities have increased by multi-folds.

As compared to India, in Britain formal music education started very early. In 1464 Cambridge University awarded first Mus B and a year later Mus D degrees. At the Oxford University the first recorded degree of B.Mus was given in 1502 and D.Mus in 1511.[2] In respect of other music activities *e.g.* music libraries, music records collections, institutions and research activities Europe and United States are far ahead of India.

Advent of Gramophone in India

The credit for sound recording and reproducing it goes to Edison who on 12 August 1877 astonished himself and others by reciting words "Mary had a little lamb" into the crude device and heard these words back. In 1898 an American introduced flat discs *i.e.* gramophone records and by 1901 commercial production of gramophone record started.

In India gramophone recording started in 1902 when T W Gainberg came to India. He used the new wax process. The first native recordings were made on 8th November 1902 by two little nautch girls aged fourteen and sixteen years.[3] In 1908, the first gramophone factory was set up at Balaghat in Kolkatta. Another large factory was established in 1928 at Dum Dum, also in Kolkatta.

Initially the Gramophone Company of India under the banner of 'HMV' and "His Master's Voice" had the monopoly over the business. The indigenous sound recording industry began in 1906 when H Bose's records hit the market followed by more Indian enterprises. These were commercial firms unconcerned with the preservation of Indian musical heritage. The British Government also failed towards its duty of establishing some kind of music archives or libraries. Early recorded music of India has been lost and whatever remains is in private custody with a high risk of being lost.

After independence some noted musicologists and the Government of India showed their consciousness and concern for the preservation of Indian music. According to Prof. R C Mehta "The great efforts to put oral traditions of music to written notations by musicologists like Bhatkhande, Vishnu Digamber Paluskar, Krishnadhan Banerjee, S M Tagore, Mudaliar and a few others could be treated as documentation and data collection of the first few decades of the twentieth century"[4]

In 1954, Government of India established All India Radio Archives at New Delhi. It was first such initiative towards preserving Indian musical heritage. It has tapes of historical, political and cultural importance and high quality recordings of classical, light and folk music. In 1984, the Central Government founded National Film Archives at Pune. It is a unique source for film music from India.

Sangeet Natak Akademi, New Delhi set up in 1953 is an institute of national importance. It is devoted to the promotion of Indian music, dance and drama and accords high priority to the building up of its archives, museums and library. It has more than 10,000 discs. Since 1981 the Akademi is engaged in video documentation of various music festivals and "holds more than 6200 hours of audio and more than 1300 hours of video recordings"[5] National Centre for the Performing Arts (Mumbai), Bharat Bhavan (Bhopal) and American Institute of Indian Studies (Gurgaon, Haryana) are some other places where music archives exist. R C Mehta has also mentioned some individuals and societies names where large quantities of gramophone records are available.

More than hundred Indian universities offer music as a subject upto post graduate levels with research. Most of these do not have separate music libraries. Here the music collection is a part of central library. The Music Department of Delhi University has a fully developed music library with separate audio-visual collection, listening room and a braille section. Some other universities *e.g.* Banaras Hindu University, Indira Kala Sangeet Vishwavidyalaya, M S University of Baroda, and Vishva Bharati include discs in their library collections.

It is evident that large quantity of recorded music is in possession of individuals, government or private organizations. This archival material is not available to the researchers because it is unorganized without catalogues, classification or printed discographies. Though central and state governments alongwith autonomous bodies have taken steps toward establishing music libraries/music archives, yet serious efforts to document the recorded music are missing. Literature guides on Indian music and library science were scanned to locate some writings on music libraries, music archives or record colletions, but nothing was found.

For better organisation of book and non-book music materials, new techniques and technologies for quick information storage and retrieval are needed. A well designed library classification scheme suitable for Indian music is drastically needed. This work is an effort to provide it.

Classification Schemes for Music Books

In the second half of sixteen century the Christian missionaries brought printing to India. The first book was printed at Goa in 1557 under the title Doctorina Christa- a religious text in Portuguese language. In the nineteenth century, the British Government introduced formal education. To meet the demand for books, commercial printing followed. Indian national movement accelerated the book publishing in vernacular languages. Towards the end of nineteenth century many music schools were established. The students needed music books. It may be assumed that birth of music book collections or music libraries took place. After independence with expansion of education, more universities with music departments were established. In India concept of music library is not very old and so no literature on music librarianship and its functioning is available.

In India the music literature generally is a section of main collection of a college, university or public library. Music books are classified, catalogued and shelved with other books. General schemes of library classification are used for classifying of books. Dewey Decimal Classification

(DDC) is an old scheme. It is good for Western music books. DDC is unsuitable for Indian music books. The librarians apply DDC schedule for music with local variations and extensions that vary from library to library. The local variations add confusion rather than to solve the problem.

Music Classification Schemes

McColvin in his book Music in Public Libraries (1965) formulated a simple classification scheme for the average public music library. For this he presented the following guiding principles.[6]

(*i*) Musical scores and books on music should be clearly distinguished because the field of music and the musical literature are not quite the same. No one shall venture on music schedule that will be quite suitable for both.

(*ii*) For all purposes, the user is the most distinctive. Subdivisions of the music must be on the convenience of the users. Music literature may be arranged according to geographical area, nationality, composers or alphabetically. But for a reader requiring information on an instrument, these shall not be helpful.

(*iii*) The third principle of music classification scheme given by McColvin is that the sequence of the schedules for music should be based as far as possible upon the evolution of the art. Attempts to carry logic and historical order too far would produce an unworkable and confused scheme. Yet it seems sensible to place first the types of music that came first and to proceed from the simple to the complex and from one to many. Accordingly it is better to place vocal music first followed by instrumental music.

For the libraries using DDC, the author had suggested (in 1924) to use capital letter M for music, or to adopt a simple method of removing the decimal point one digit forward *e.g.* 78.2 for operas and 782 for books on operas.

E J Coates Music Classification Scheme

British Catalogue of Music which has been compiled by E J Coates used a faceted scheme of classification and so was capable of representing each characteristic of music. An example from this scheme is given. A book 'Selection from South Pacific arranged for accordion solo' shall be assigned classification number as RSPMK/CM/J R which may be broken as.[7]

R	organ
RS	... Accordion
RSPM	... Unaccompanied accordion solo
RSPMK	... Arrangements
RSPMK/CM	... from musical plays
RSPMK/CM/JR	... Film music

At a time when the librarians were accustomed to numerical notation of DDC, Coates introduced alphabetical notation. In DDC mnemonic feature are easily recognized but in Coates scheme these are little and unrecognizable. Coates has framed faceted classification. He has used round brackets to denote common form of subdivisions and by using oblique stroke further subdivisions are shown. There are seven auxiliary tables for various purposes. About Coates classification for music books Jack Dove said "for a large music collection where minute classification illustrating various aspects is called for this scheme has every thing in its favour."[8]

Library Classification Schemes for Music by Indians

As said earlier, schedules for western music are well developed in general classification schemes as DDC, Library of Congress (LC) and special schemes as given by McColvin and Coates. But none of these have provisions for Indian music. Indeed it is impossible to use any of these schemes for classifying Indian music literature.[9]

T N Rajan has used Dr. Ranganathan methodology for developing a full schedule for Indian music. He has used Roman small and capital letters with Indo-Arabic numerals. Small Roman letters have been used for common subdivisions, capital Roman letters for facets and Indo-Arabic numerals for further dividing the facets. Some classification number based on this schedule are

Indian Music	8 H A
Karnatak Music	8 H A 1
Dictionary of Karnataka Music	8 H A 1 1 6
Violin (Karnatak Music)	8 H A 1 E 2 1 2 1

(Digit 8 is for music literature)

B C Deva, a noted musicologists has designed a schedule for "classification of Indian musical instruments."[10] It is based on DDC but may be used by librarians in any classification scheme. The author has listed music instruments in details.

Categories of Music

An Indian musicologist has divided music into five categories. According to him these "music categories are fundamental classes in which the totality of music material of any society can be naturally organized. The categorizations, because of its naturalness, reflects corresponding genera of kinds of experience received from different music." These categories are:

1. Primitive or tribal music
2. Folk music
3. Devotional music

4. Art (or classical) music
5. Popular music

About above categories, Ashok Ranade further writes that "Each category poses a variety of questions and necessitates formulations of conceptual framework of disparate philosophical import."[11] Later on in his another book this author realized that there exists a sixth category of music also. This category is confluence of music or fusion music.[12]

Colon Cassification

Dr. Ranganathan in his Colon Classification 6th edition (CC6) has given schedule for music under N R (pages 1.97 and 2.93). It is as follows:

NR[P1], [P2]] [P3]; [M]: [E cum 2P]. Here P is got by geographical device (GD) as NR 44 Indian music. P 2 is assigned by chronological device (CD). To assign a class number to a style (P2) as dhrupad or khayal or a gharana, it is almost impossible to locate its origin. Similarly under P3 music has been enumerated. Music from India or any region cannot be limited to seven entities. Instruments have been listed under matter 'M'. Here too western music instruments dominate the list. Flute and vina are Indian, harmonium, drums and violin are Indian as well as western. Rests are western music instruments.

Librarians using CC6, face difficulties for classifying the Indian music books. Schedule given by Ranganathan is insufficient. Classifiers amend and expand the schedule according to their needs. There is no uniformity. So there is drastic need to design an expanded version of NR as part of CC6. This will help all the librarians using CC6 for classification.

REFERENCES

1. Abbasi, N A and M L Saini. Manuscript wealth of India. *In*. Gupta, B B. Handbook of libraries, archives and information centres. Vol. 2, Delhi; Information Industry Pub; 1986. p. 490.
2. New Grove Dictionary of Music and Musician. Vol. 2, p. 6.
3. Kinnear, Michael. The Gramophone Company's first Indian recordings.1899-1903 Bombay; Popular Prakashan, 1994. p. 11.
4. Mehta, R C. Indian classical music and gharana traditions. New Delhi; Readworthy, 2008. p. 113.
5. *Ibid*. p. 116.
6. Jack, Dove. Music Libraries. Vol. 1, London; Andre Deutsch, 1965. p. 48-49.
7. *Ibid*. p. 66.
8. *Ibid*. p. 66.
9. Rajan, T N. Classification scheme for Indian music literature. *Sangeet Natak*. No. 16, June 1970. p. 74.
10. Deva, BC. Classification of Indian musical instruments. *Journal of the Indian Musicological Society*. January 1973, Vol. 4, No. 1, p. 33-45.
11. Ranade, Ashok D. Essays in Indian ethnomusicology. New Delhi; Munshiram Manoharlal, 1998. p. 1.
12. Ranade, Ashok D. Perspective on music: Ideas and theories. New Delhi; Promila, 2008. p. 6.

2

Expanded Schedules: Organology

Genesis

In 1986, the author joined the Music Department library, University of Delhi, as Incharge. The library had about 8000 books on music and other subjects. All and these were unclassified. Firstly DDC 18 was used for classifying the music books. Soon it was evident that for Indian music books, DDC 18 is not a workable classification scheme. Later on Colon Classification, ed 6 (CC6) was used for this job. But here the music schedule for music under NR is very brief. It does not enumerate in details the music instruments and forms of Indian vocal music. There was drastic need to expand it in such a way that it becomes a part of the host scheme *i.e.* CC6 so that the libraries using it are benefitted.

Methodology

Dr. Ranganathan has provided full details for designing of depth classification schedules for existing and new emerging subjects. This method has been further discussed by the authors writing books on theory of library science. For designing this expanded music schedule under CC6, Ranganathan's guidelines have been followed with necessary deviations.

Laboratory for Designing and Testing

The Music Department library which is a division of Delhi University Library System, now has about 15000 books on music and allied subjects in English, Hindi, Tamil, Sanskrit and other Indian languages. These include music bibliographies, subject dictionaries, subject encyclopaedias and language dictionaries. So sufficient music literature was available. This was supplemented by author's published music bibliography that included information about 4000 books, articles and theses. The teaching faculty in the Music Department, University of Delhi, is one of the best in India. They happily assisted and guided. The draft schedules were prepared as follows.

1. In the beginning the titles of about two hundred books in English and Hindi were collected from the library catalogue. These were supplemented by another hundred ones from the author's music bibliography.

2. From the above cards the details *e.g.* terms, ideas, forms of music, names of music instruments, gharanas, ragas etc. were noted on paper slips. The explanations and relationship of these entities with other terms were explained.

3. These slips were arranged in descending order of the main subject and its divisions. The author has the practical experience of arranging books on shelves. He has compiled two music bibliographies where the entries are arranged in broad chapters further divided into headings and sub headings.

4. Indian music is a fast expanding subject. It has manifested itself into many directions. Indian universities have separate departments for Hindustani music (vocal), Karnataka music (vocal) instrumental music (Karnataka and Hindustani)

Rabindra Sangeet and folk music. All of these divisions of Indian music cannot be accommodated in one schedule. So the following schedules have been drafted.

MNR	Organology (Music instruments making)
NR	Music—General and vocal
NRV	Instrumental music
NRY	Folk music (Ethnomusicology)

The above schedules are expansion in canonical sequences of NR (music) in CC6. All the tables, devices, divisions of CC6 are to be used as directed by Dr. Ranganathan. The author has only expanded and enumerated in details majority of the ideas, concepts, forms of music and musical instruments.

5. Once, the draft schedules for vocal music, instrumental music, folk music and organology were ready, these were tested by classifying the books available in the Music Department library. Necessary changes, additions, deletions and relocations were carried out and the final draft was completed.

ORGANOLOGY

(Music Instrument Making)

By Dr. Ranganathan music instrument making has been assigned the canonical class MNR. This needs further expansion. So under new heading organology this class has been fully developed. This class deals primarily with music instruments, and so these have been assigned the status of personality (P1) and the parts of the instruments have been allotted [P2]. All the instruments are made of some materials. So under the category matter, the material used is placed. All these have been enumerated.

[E cum 2P] has not been enumerated. The space, wherever necessary shall be shown in the last by (S). The schedule is as.

MNR [P1], [P2]; [M] : [E Cum 2P]. S

P1 as P1 of NRV

[P2]

1	**Parts and accessories**
11	Decoration
12	By paintings
13	By engraving
14	By pasting
2	**Parts mainly used for solid music instruments**
3	**Parts mainly used for percussion instruments**
31	Khaal (skin parchment)
32	Gajra/Singar (a leather ring with holes)
33	Baddhi/Tasma (braces made of leather)
34	Gatta/Addu (small wooden blocks)
36	Aindy/Ring (for balancing the instrument)
38	Hammer
4	**Parts mainly used for wind instruments**
42	Tube/Nay
5	**Parts used for string instruments**
51	Tumba
511	Khoonti (pegs)
52	Peg box
521	Frets
523	Tarb
53	Chikari (drove strings)
531	Finger board
534	Jawari/Bridge
54	Tabli
55	Strings
551	Langot (string holder)
553	Manaka (fine tuner)
56	Parchment (skin/leather)
58	Mizrab (striker)

6	**Parts mainly used for key board instruments**
61	Box
63	Reeds
65	Parda (wooden plank)
67	Dhamman
	Foci in [M]
1	**General materials**
11	Diamond
12	Other costly stones
2	**Natural products**
21	Wood
211	Bomboo
22	Jute
24	Cotton
26	Reed
28	Coconut shell
3	Animal products
31	Leather
33	Bone
35	Horn
36	Conch
37	Ivory
4	**Metals**
41	Iron
411	Steel
42	Copper
421	Bronze
43	Silver
44	Gold
5	**Man made products**
51	Ink
511	Colours
514	Paints
52	Paper
54	Plastics
56	Adhesive
58	Polish

3

Vocal Music

This schedule is the main. In addition to vocal music books, the general books on music *e.g.* history of music, gharanas, religious music etc. shall be classified here. For drafting it, the sample was available in abundance. With the help of this the cards were arranged in descending order of the entities. The author had the practical experience of arranging the concepts in helpful sequence. So preparing the first draft for vocal music was easy. With the help of this draft schedule, about two hundred titles in Hindi and English language were classified and the final schedule for vocal music was prepared.

In CC6, P1 of NR is got by geographical division (GD) and P2 is got by chronological device (CD). To determine the date of origin for a music style *e.g.* khayal, thumri, raga etc. cannot be estimated. So, forms of vocal music cannot be shown by using CD. For this a detailed enumeration of facets was needed and has been given. The P2 starts with theory of music followed by sound. Both of these are root of the subject. After sound in facet 3 raga has been placed. Forms of vocal music are covered under two sections of the facets form. First half section deals with Hindustani music and the second half with Karnatak music.

Gharana system is a unique institution of music that exists in India only. The other countries do not have anything like gharana. To classify it with GD and CD is a logical idea given by Ranganathan. But practically it is very difficult to find the place of origin with date. If one succeeds in finding both then the class number shall be very long. For example it is very difficult to know the place of origin for Senia Gharana and Bhindi Bazar Gharana. To make the notation brief and simple alphabetical device has been used. It shall be helpful for classifier and the reader.

NR[P1], P2; [M]: [E cum 2P]

P1 by Geographic device

Foci in [P2]

1	**Theory/Musicology**
11	Language of music
12	Voice
13	Voice culture
14	Acoustics
15	Prabandh
16	Compositions
161	Geetak
162	Geeti
	By subject as
16(0153)	Punjabi compositions
18	Notation
181	Staff notation
183	Indian systems of notations
1831	Notation by ancient authors
1832	Notation by medieval authors
184	Notation by modern authors
1841	By Pt. Paluskar
1842	By Pt. Bhatkhande
1843	By post Bhatkhande authors
1844	Notation in Braille script
2	**Sound (Nada)**
22	Swara

221 Types of swara
222 Shudh swara
223 Komal swara
224 Teevra swara
225 Vadi swara
226 Samvadi swara
227 Anuwadi swara
228 Vivadi swara

23 Grama

231 Shadja grama
232 Madhyam grama
233 Gandharva grama
234 Murchna
235 Jati
236 Mela
237 Varna
238 Alankar

24 Rhythm (Laya)

25 Tala
251 Units of tala
2511 Matra
2512 Akshara
252 Talganas
2521 Anudrats
2522 Druts
2523 Lagu
2524 Guru
2525 Pluta
2526 Kakapada
253 Sapta tala
2531 Dhruva
2532 Matya
2533 Rupaka
2534 Jhampa
2535 Triputa
2536 Ata
2537 Eka
255 Tala Jati
2551 Tisra

2552 Chatusra
2553 Khanda
2554 Misra
2555 Sankirna

26 Pitch

261 Timpre (Quality)
27 Intensity
271 Duration
28 Gamaka
281 Panchadasa gamaka
282 Rayodasa
283 Dasa Vidha Gamaka

3 Raga

31 Raga classification systems
32 Time theory
321 Jati system
322 Suddha-chayalaga
323 Raga-ragini parivar system
324 Janaka-Janya system
3241 Varjya Vakra
3242 Upanga Bhasha Ang
3244 Ragaang system
3246 Gram raga vargikaran
3248 Male raga vargikaran
35 That raga system

351 Bilawal
352 Kalyan
353 Khamaj
354 Bhairav
355 Poorvi
356 Bhairavi
357 Asavari
358 Kafi
3591 Todi
3592 Sarang
3593 Malhar
3594 Kanhra

36	Melakarta system
	(Sampurna Mela Paddhiti)
361	Indu
362	Notra
363	Agni
364	Veda
365	Bana
366	Ritu
367	Rishi
368	Vasa
3691	Brahma
3692	Disi
3693	Rudra
3694	Aditya
4	**Forms of music (Hindustani)**
41	Dhrupad
411	Dhamar
412	Khayal
413	Hori
414	Haveli sangeet
42	Thumri
421	Dadra
422	Tappa
423	Tarana
424	Sadra
425	Tirvat
426	Chaturang
4261	Lakshan geet
43	Alap
431	Sargam
432	Sargam geet
433	Tana
45	**Forms of music (Karnatak)**
451	Manodharma sangit
4511	Raag alapana
4514	Madhyama kala or tana
452	Pallavi

4521	Sahitya prastara or niraval
4522	Svara kalpana
453	Kalpita sangit
4531	Svaravali
4532	Alankaram
4533	Geet
4534	Suladi
4535	Svarajati
4536	Jati svaram
4537	Varnam
45371	Tana varnam
45372	Pada varnam
454	Kirtis
4541	Group kirtis
455	Kirtans
4551	Padam
4552	Jawali
4553	Daru
4554	Tillana
5	**Other forms of vocal music**
51	Patriotic songs
52	Light music
522	Ghazal
53	Qawwali
54	Songs
	(Others by subject device)
5 (Δ25)	Bhakti sangeet
5 (Δ73)	Sufiana kalam
5 (Q)	Religious songs
5 (Q 2)	Bhajans
5 (Q 7)	Naats/Hamds
5 (Q 8441)	Kirtan (Sikh)
5 (NW)	Film songs
6	**Gharanas**
	(To be arranged alphabetically as)
6 A	Agra
6 A J	Ajrara

6 B	Banaras
6 BH	Bhindi Bazar
6 D	Delhi
6 G	Gwalior
6 I	Indore
6 J	Jaipur
6 K	Kirana
6 P	Patiala
6 R	Rampur
6 S	Sainia
6 V	Vishnupur
7	**Western music (to be enumerated)**
8	**Western music (to be enumerated)**
9	**Special types of music**
91	Theatre music
92	Drama music
93	Opera
94	Ballet
NR ( )	**Types of music**
NR(O157)	Rabindra sangeet
NR (Q2)	Hindu music
NR (Q5)	Christian music
NR (Y54)	Military music

Foci in [M]

1	**Gramophone records**
11	78 RMP (3 minutes)
12	45 RMP (5 minutes)
14	L P
2	**Spools**
21	Audio cassettes
22	Audio visual cassette
3	**Compact Disc**
31	A C D
32	V C D
34	D V D
36	Computer CD

Foci in E cum 2 P

1. Riaz (Practising)
2. Listening
3. Stage performance
4. Recordings

4

Instrumental Music

The variety of music instruments in India is enormous. Indians use ancient music instruments as well as modern electronic music instruments. Moreover all types of instrumental music is getting popular. All music educational institutions usually have at least two separate departments-one for vocal music and the other for instrumental music. These factors compel the librarians for considering the instrumental music as a fully developed discipline and shelve these books separately.

The music instruments may be divided in groups on the basis of origin, material used, mode of playing and many more. The Chinese have classified their music instruments into eight groups on the basis of the nature of material used. In Europe too, numerous music instruments classification schemes have been evolved. But all these do not suit the Indian ones.

In India many musicologists *e.g.* Kohala, Narad and Bharat (Natyasastra) have classified the music instruments. Bharata has divided these into four categories. This is a good classification scheme and suits Dr. Ranganathan theory of library classification. So the music instruments have been grouped according to Bharat's principles with modifications *e.g.* electronic music instruments.

Dr. Ranganathan has categorized the music instruments as 'matter'. If this is accepted, then all the books on music instruments shall scatter to various places. The scholar shall like to see all the books on a particular instrument placed at one place in the book shelf. Recently a book namely 'Sitar compositions' by Dr. Anupam Mahajan has been published. If sitar is considered as 'matter' the class no shall be as: Music, India, Composition, Sitar. In the shelf this book shall be kept with books on music compositions and not with books on sitar. Similarly there are many books on violin related with Karnataka music, Hindustani music or Western music. These books hall be scattered at three different places. To resolve this dilemma, a small sample of one hundred titles on instrumental music was selected and classified by treating music instruments as personality as well as matter. Finally the result showed that all the documents on particular music instrument should be shelved at one place alongwith its family. So, music instruments have been enumerated under personality category.

Once the draft schedule was ready, it was further tested by classifying more documents and shortcomings were removed. India has large variety of music instruments. All of these have not been enumerated. To accommodate new, gaps have been provided. In each category of music instruments digits upto 5 or 6 have been used. Gaps have been left for further enumeration of western music instruments.

The twentieth century has been a century of inventions and new discoveries. "The rapid and revolutionary advances in the field of micro electronics paved the way for phenomenal progress in the field of musical instruments in recent times."[1] Initially we had electric instruments that meant music instruments whose sound was produced mechanically and only amplified or altered electronically *e.g.* electric guitar. An electronic instrument may include a user interface for controlling its sound, often by adjusting the pitch, frequency, or duration of each note. Now electronic music instruments are widely used in European and American countries. The development of new electronic musical instruments, controller and synthesizers is the result of continuing serious interdisciplinary research. Due to this more and more improved versions of synthesizers are coming to the markets.

In India, musicians use electronic musical instruments in light music programmes. As far as classical music concerned, these are in little use. Indian authors writing books on Indian music instruments have not discussed electric or electronic music instruments. Prof. Suneera Kasliwal is perhaps the first Indian author who has devoted one chapter to such music instruments. She has furnished details of some electronic musical instruments that are being used for Indian classical music concerts. Some of these are Saarang (electronic tanpura), Dhruva (electronic surpeti) and Taanmala (electronic tabla).

The electronic musical instruments differ with traditional one. The following differences make them a class itself.

(a) These are electricity based.
(b) Most of these have keyboards as input device.
(c) These consist on very complicated electronic system.
(d) These are manufactured/repaired by technical persons.
(e) An important difference is that these are undergoing fast changes in size, design, and internal systems. (circuits)

The books related with electronic musical systems should be placed with instrumental music, but with a difference. For such literature digit 7 has been assigned in the personality. This shall be divided further with class number of the instruments. NRV 7 is for general books on electronic music instruments. 71 has been left blank and arrays from 72 to 76 have been assigned to electronic music instruments as

733	Electronic tabla
752	Electronic tanpura
7523	Electronic guitar

Digits from 77 onwards has left unused for further expansion.

INSTRUMENTAL MUSIC
NRV [P1], [P2]; [M]: [E CUM 2P]. S

Foci in [P1]

1	**Music instruments** (General works)
12	Classification of music instruments
2	**Solids (Ghana vadyas)**
21	Bells
213	Ghanta
214	Ghoongroo
244	Manjeera
245	Thali
246	Chimta
254	Danda
255	Rings
256	Kartar
26	Jaltarang
27	Pots
28	Plates
29	Rods
3	**Percussion instruments (Avanadha vadyas)**
31	Daff/Daffali
311	Patacha
312	Kanjira
313	Moorchang
33	Tabla
331	Nagara/Naqqara

332 Tasa
34 Dholak
35 Pakhawaj
351 Mridangam
352 Khole
36 Drums
361 Damru
362 Ghatam
363 Matki

4 Wind instruments (Sushira vadyas)
41 Flutes
411 Transverse flute
412 Vertical flute
413 Conch
414 Algoza
42 Turahi
43 Shehnai
431 Pongi
432 Nadaswaram
44 Trumphetes
441 Bugles
45 Horn and like these brass instruments
451 Clarinet
454 Whistles
46 Tuba
461 Oboe
462 Saxaphone

5 String instruments (Tatya vadyas)
51 Tanpura
511 Veena
512 Vichitra veena
513 Rudra veena
514 Tanjauri veena
515 Saraswati veena
516 Kinnari
517 Ektantri
52 Sitar
521 Lute
522 Mandolin

523	Guitar
524	Surbahar
53	Sarod
531	Sursingar
532	Rabab
5321	Kashmiri rabab
5322	Hindustani rabab
533	Gottuvadyam
54	Sarangi
541	Esraj
542	Tausa
55	Violin
551	Viola
556	Dilruba
558	Santoor
56	Bango
6	**Keyboard instruments**
61	Harmonium
62	Piano
621	Banjo
64	Casio
7	**Electronic music instruments**
	(to be divided by the music instruments from 2 to 6 as)
733	Electronic tabla
752	Electronic tanpura
7523	Electronic guitar
8	**Instrumental music**
82	Symphony
821	Band music
822	Military band
83	Orchestra/vrindagam/Kutapsa
831	Jugalbandi
832	Taal katcheri
84	Jazz
85	Concerts
86	Chamber music
862	Duets
863	Trios

864	Quartets
865	Quintet
866	Sixtets
869	Octets
8692	Nonet and larger combination

P2	to be taken from P1 of NR (Vocal music)
E cum 2P	to be taken from E cum 2P of NR (Vocal music)

REFERENCE

1. Kasliwal, Suneera. Classical musical instruments. New Delhi; Rupa & Co., 2001. p. 290.

5

Folk Music

The notion that there exists something like folk music as distinct from other types of music is accepted in European and American countries. In other parts of the world, folk music had little recognition. In 1955, at an international conference folk music not only was accepted as a separate category of music but also was defined as "Folk music is the product of a musical tradition that has been evolved through the process of oral transmission. The factors that shape the tradition are *(i)* Continuity that links the present with past. *(ii)* Variation which springs from the creative impulse of the individual or the group. *(iii)* Selection by the community which determines the form or forms in which the music survives."[1]

The above definition applies to music that has been evolved from rudimentary beginnings by a community. It is oral and unwritten living tradition of a community. Modern society is industrial where information technology and new media play vital role for folk music. Emphasis on oral transmission of music tradition is good but sophisticated music systems are indispensable part of modern music environment. Due to these changes folk music has acquired a new concept and wide dimensions.

Ethnomusicology is another growing subject that is related with folk and tribal music. The term ethnomusicology was coined in 1950 by Jaap Kunst. Later on this term was used by many European authors. Today "ethnomusicology is concerned primarily with living music (and musical instruments and dance) of oral tradition, outside the limits of urban art music.[2] Here the chief objects of investigation are the music of non literate people (or tribal music's), the orally transmitted music of high cultures of Asia and folk music.

Only a few Indian universities offer folk music as subject. The state governments and state academies encourage projects or publications related with folklore of their state. Folk musicians are also given state patronage. Abundant literature is available on folk music. Ethnomusicology is an emerging subject which is interlinked with 'folk music'. In Europe and United States it has been recognized as a discipline but in India it is not the case. The librarians classify the folk music books either under NR by using subject device or under folklore Y. These are scattered at various places. So there is a need to provide a canonical class number to it and shelf all such books at one place. This will benefit the researchers.

It is evident that CC6 is insufficient for classifying the folk music books. The expanded schedule of NR failed to classify the exiting books in Music Department Library. These books were scattered at many places. So to provide all material at one place, the schedule for Folk Music (NRY) was designed. As ethnomusicology and folk music are very close to each other, the books on ethnomusicology will be classified under folk music.

For constructing the schedule, the ideas, concepts, terms and materials used by folk artists were collected from the books available in Music Department library. By analyzing these, it was found that the literature contained information about

(*a*) Geographical area to which the folk music belongs.

(*b*) Music as sound, compositions, folk geet and rhythm etc.
(*c*) Music instruments used by folk artists.
(*d*) Occasions when this music is played or songs are sung.
(*e*) Ornaments and dresses used by these artistes.

For finalizing the proposed schedule, NR (Vocal music) and NRV (Instrumental music) were ready. For enumerating the activities, dress, ornaments and occasions, the model from E cum 2P of Y (sociology) has been taken. The new schedule for folk music is given below.

NRY [P1], [P2]; [M]: [E cum 2P]

P1	Area from which folk music belongs. To be taken from Geographical Division.
P2	As P2 of NR Vocal music.
M	Matter to be taken from P1 NRV music instruments.

E cum 2 P

1	**Culture/civilization**
11	Features
3	**Activities**
31	Ceremonies
312	Birth
313	Naming
314	Birthday
315	Wedding
32	Funeral
321	Post funeral
351	Folklore
356	Customs
36	Festivals
36 (Q)	Religious ceremonies
36 (Q2)	Hindu festivals
38	Symbolism

4	**Preservation**
86	**Ornaments** (may be divided as 1 of (P) of L medicine) as
8631	Toe rings
8633	Anklets
8637	Waist cord
8666	Bangles
8667	Necklace
8668	Ring
8683	Ear rings
8684	Head wear/crown
8697	Tattooing
88	Dress
881	Costumes
883	For lower parts *e.g.*' skirts, paint
884	for Abdomen *e.g.* shirts, salwar coat
888	for upper body *e.g.* cap, scarf
8881	face masks

REFERENCES

1. Folk music. Grove Dictionary of Music and Musicians, Vol. 6. p. 693.
2. *Ibid.*, p. 275-281.

6

Schedules Index

7

Classified Sample of Music Literature

24(NR);128:8	Sound archives./ Mohammed Haroon.
MNR.44	Indian organology./B C Deva.
MNR:g	Problems and aspects of reconstruction of musical instruments./Nellyvan Dee Bernard.
MNR1.44:g(A)	Scientific problems in the construction of musical instruments./S D Ramanathan.
MNR51,534-55	Some studies on spectral dynamics of tanpura strings with relation to perception of jawari./R Sengupta.
MNR51,55	Acoustics signal processing of a tanpura string in different time segments./R Sengupta.
MNR52,55v	Musical evolution related to sitara strings./ S Rao.
NA44:(NR)	Music and architecture./G F Winckel.
NA44,8(NR)	An ideal concert hall./G Kuppuswami.
ND44:g(NRV)	Musical instruments in Indian arts./S Krishnaswami.

ND4437:g(NRV)	Musical instruments as represented in sculptures of Rajasthan./ Neelima Vashishtha.
NROaΔ : 36	Music and meditation./Diana Dunningham.
NROaNRY:g	Folk and classical music: a dichotomy that does not quite work in India./ Mukund Lath.
NROaQ7	Music in Islam./M L Roychoudhury.
NR44aN9	Music literature from India./ Mohammed Haroon.
NR44k	Living idioms in Hindustani music./ Pandit Amarnath.
NR44v'C	Music and musical thought in early India./Lewis Rowell.
NR44xl,1	Sangit Ratnakara./Sharangdeva.
NR44x3,1	Brhaddesi./Matanga.
NR44x4,1	Sangeet Samay Saar./Parsava Deva.
NR44x5,1	Sangeet Makaranda./Narada.
NR44x5,2	Naradiya shiksha mein sangeet./ Manish Dangwal.
NR44x6,1	Bharat Bhashyam./Nanya Bhoopal.
NR44xF29,1	Manasollas./Someshvar.
NR44xI33	Sangeet Raj./Maharana Kumbha.
NR44xJ00,1	Raag Tarangini./Lochan.
NR44xJ20,1	Svara Mela kala nidhi./Ramamatya.
NR44xJN,41x	A compilation of dhrupada texts

	ascribed to Bakshoo./ Prem Lata Sharma.
NR44xK00,1	Sangeet Darpan./Damodar.
NR44xK,12,1	Sangeet Parijata./Ahobala.
NR44xK90,1	Sangeet Damodar./Shubankar.
NR44xL89,1	Sangeet Raghunandnam./Wisvanath Dev.
NR44xM60,1	Sangeet Sastra./V N Bhatkhande.
NR44xM60,2	Sri Mallaksha Sangeetam./V N Bhatkhande.
NR44xM60,3	Kramik pustak malika./V N Bhatkhande.
NR44xM60,5	Sangeet paddhtiyo ka tulnatamak adhyayan./V N Bhatkhande.
NR44xM60,6	Svar malika./V N Bhatkhande.
NR44xN00,1	Taan sangraha./S N Ratanjankar.
NR44xN00,2	Abhinav sangeet shiksha./S N Ratanjankar.
NR44xN00,3	Abhinav geet manjari,/S N Ratanjankar.
NR44xN00,6	Taal lakshan geet sangraha./S N Ratanjankar.
NR44xN11,3	Maarifun naghmaat./Raja Nawab Ali.
NR44y^{7}I80	Swami Haridas—Father of Hindustani music./K J Iyengar.
NR44y^{7}J06	Sangeet Samarat, Tansen./Susheela Mishra.
NR 44 y^7 J06, 41 'N K (O1521 is	Tansen and the tradition of dhrupad songs in the Braj language from the

for Braj language)	16th century to the present day./ Francoise Delvoye.
NR44y^7 M60	Bhatkhande's contribution to music./ Sobhana Nayar.
NR44y^7 M60,42	Pandit Bhatkhande's thought on thumri./Prabhakar Chinchore.
NR44y^7 M72	Pandit Vishnu Digambar Paluskar./ V R Athavale.
NR44y^8	Bhartiya sangeet sangrah./S K Goswami.
NR44y^8	Lakshanagranthas in music./S Bhagyalakshmi.
NR44z^7	Essays in musicology./R C Mehta.
NR44	Music culture of India./V K Narayan Menon.
NR440aA	Music and science./B C Deva.
NR440aC5:3	Laser spectroscopy and basic aspects of Indian music.
NR440aΔ73	Sufism and music./N P Ahmad.
NR440a0	Sahitya sangeet aur kala./Komal Kothari.
NR440a0	Sahitya and sangeeta./V Wamanam
NR440aQ:415	Music and symbolism./Ashok D Ranade.
NR440aQ2:23	Music and tantras./M R Gautam.
NR440aQ23:22	Puranas and music./Alain Danielou.
NR440aS	Sangeet evam manovigyan./Kiran Tiwari.

NR440aSM	Experimental psychology and Indian music./K G Virmani.
NR44OaY	Bhartiya sanskriti shaswat jeewan drishti evam sangeet./Ruchi Gupta.
NR44OaY	Music and society./Sunita Dhar.
NR44OaY:3	Music and the Indian yoga./R F Bruckner.
NR44ObL:4	Music and healing./Rayasree Bandyopadhyay.
NR44ObΔ25	Bhakti and music./N Pattabhi Raman.
NR44ObO15	The role of Sanskrit in the development of Indian music./S S Janaki.
NR44ObQ:1	Music and mythology./R C Mehta.
NR44ObR5	Aesthetics of Indian music./A A Banke.
NR44ObR5	Rasa theory and Indian music./ Premlata Sharma.
NR44ObR635	The spiritual influence of yoga activity on Indian music./Padma Sudhi.
NR44ObX	Adhunik vyasaik Hindustani shastriya gayan./Jeet Ram Sharma.
NR44ObX8(A)	Effects of industralisation on music./ K L Sondhi.
NR44ObY	Social function of Indian music./ M R Gautam.
NR44ObY	Role of music in society and culture./S Bhattacharya.
NR44ObY51	Royal patronage to Indian music./ Gowry Kuppuswamy.

NR44ObY592	Our Indian classical music and castes./ B Mohala.
NR44OcQ'J	Madhya kaleen dharma mein shastriya sangeet ka tulnatamak adhyayan./J H Khanna.
NR44Oj5	East meets west./Gayatri Chandrashekhar.
NR44Oj5,211	Development of Indian and western musical scales./Gowry Kuppuswamy.
NR44Oj5,24	Indian and western rhythm./Temple T Tutte.
NR44Oj5,452	Western parallel of Indian Pallavi techniques./E Te Nigenhuis.
NR44Om5	Indian and western music structural differences and similarities./Manfred Junius.
NR44'N6	Music; New influence and changes./B C Deva.
NR44'N8	Current trends in Hindustani music./ Sudha Mathur.
NR44.72	Indian music in America./Joan Mubayi.
NR44:g	Appreciating India's music./ Emmons E White.
NR44:g	The 'modern', the 'traditional' and 'criticism' in the Indian musical tradition./Mukund Lath.
NR44:g	Condemnation and appreciation of arts./Debashree Bhattacharya.
NR44:g	Indian music: Problems and prospects./B V Leskar.

NR44:g(O,1)	Poetry in Indian classical music. /G N Joshi.
NR44:g(Y:86)	Bhartiya sangeet mein alankar./ Shabnam.
NR44:(A)	Science in and of music./Santimay Chatterjee.
NR44:(B)	Mathematics of music./Harikant Shukla.
NR44:(G)	Bio evolution of man and music./ Prerna Chawla.
NR44:(R)	Philosophy of Indian music./ Satyanarayanan Panda.
NR44:(R)	Philosophy of music./Ritwik Sanyal.
NR44:(S)ObT13	Psychology of music and its bearing on child's education./ E S Perera.
NR44;1v	A concise history of the phonograph industry in India./G N Joshi.
NR44,1	Music and musicology. E S Prem Lata Sharma.
NR44,12	Training in voice and speech. One Indian approach./Ashok D Ranade.
NR44,13	Voice culture./S A K Durga.
NR44,14	Acoustic of music./W T Parlholomew.
NR44,142	Change in arts. Recent trends in Hindustani music; an appraisal./ V H Deshpande.
NR44,144	Appreciating Indian music./E E White.
NR44,145	Music criticism in India./Chetan Karnani.

NR44,15	A note on giti gana and prabandha: Compositional styles of ancient music./ G H Tarlekar.
NR44,16x	Sangeet raga kalpadrum: Encyclopaedia of Indian music./ Nagendra Nath Vasu.
NR44,16:g	Questions regarding compositions./ S K Nair.
NR44,16(0152)	Sangeetagyon kaviyon kee Hindi rachnayen./Dharmeshwar Chaturvedi.
NR44,16(0153)	Punjabi bhasha mein khyal kee paramparik bandishen./Geeta Paintal.
NR44,18:g	The adverse effect of notating ragas./ Uma Kant.
NR44,181	A handbook of staff notation for Indian music./Howard Boat Wright.
NR44,183v	History of Indian music notation system./Ram Avtar Veer.
NR44,183	Indian notation system./ Publication Division, Government of India.
NR44,1843	Musical notation in pictorial form./S V Vadnerkar.
NR44,1843Ok3	Fundamentals of raga tala with a new system of notation./Nikhil Ghosh.
NR44,2	Sounds of music./T N Seshagopalan.
NR44,2	Dhvani-Nature and culture of sound./ S C Malik.
NR44,2Oj3ObNRV	Svar aur ragon ke vikas mein vadyo ka yogdan./Indrani Chakravarti.

NR44,21	Bhartiya sangeet mein sruti./ Yashpal Sharma.
NR44,21	Sruti theory of Indian music./D D Bhate.
NR44,21:g	Problem of continuity in music and sruti./B C Deva.
NR44,21:g	Propriety of dividing octave into twenty two sruties./H V Modak.
NR44,211	Indian musical scale./Abdul Karim Khan.
NR44,22	Avenues to a svara./S K Saxena.
NR44,221	Vadi, samvadi, vivadi and anuvadi svaras./N Ramanathan.
NR44,24	Indian concept of rhythm./A K Sen.
NR44,24	Concept of laya in Hindustani music./ S K Saxena.
NR44,24Oj3	Laya in a raga./R Visweswaran.
NR44,24Oj52	The concept of tala in semi classical music./Peter Manuel.
NR44,25x	Taal kosh./G C Srivastava.
NR44,25Oj3	Evolution of raga and tala in Indian music./M R Gautam.
NR44,271	On musical intervals./Lila Ray.
NR44,28	Gamakas./C S Pant.
NR44,3v	The origin of raga./S Bandyopadhyay.
NR44,3y8	Hindustani raga index./Patrick Moutal.
NR44,3y8	Raga dhana. An alpha numerical directory of ragas./Ludwig Pesch.

NR44,3	Acceptability of new ragas in Hindustani music./Mohan Nadkarni.
NR44,3OaS	A study in the psychological response to ragas./B C Deva.
NR44,3ObO	The importance of sahitya in raga music./B Dayananda Rao.
NR44,3ObR5	Raag and rasa./P K Dixit.
NR44,3OcO	Matching of sahitya and raga./B N Chettiar.
NR44,3'M	Ragas in the nineteenth century./ Varrier Elwin.
NR44,3:g	Ragas—Right or wrong./Deepak Raja.
NR44,3:(A)	Application of new scientific method to creation of Hindustani ragas./S Chakraborty.
NR44,3:(R5)	Raga—Its aesthetics and its unfoldment through compositions./ M R Ganguli.
NR44,31	Entropy of information as a method of raga classification./K R Rajagopalan.
NR44,32	Time measurement and compositional types in Indian music./Subhadra Chaudhary.
NR44,32	Time theory in Hindustani classical music./Krishna Bisht.
NR44,32	Sandhi prakash raga./Priyanka Koshal.
NR44,321	Reconstruction of jatis./K C D Brahaspati.
NR44,322	Hindustani sangeet mein chhayalag

	evam sankirna ragon kee avadharna./ Bharti Sharma.
NR44,323	Ragas and raginis./O C Ganguli.
NR44,324	Janya ragas: Their numbers./T S Ramakrishnan.
NR44,324	Janak ragas and janya ragas./S Rajam.
NR44,3242	Classification of ragas : Raganga, bhasanga, kriayanga and upanga./ S Seetha.
NR44,3244	Significance of raganga in Hindustani music./Krishna Bisht.
NR44,35	Hindustani sangeeth: Thats./A Suridasan.
NR44,35Ot6	Bhartiya sangeet mein mela athva that ka aitihasik adhyayan./ Shoba Mathur.
NR44,354	Bhairav ke prakar./J T Shah.
NR44,356	Shastriya sangeet mein raga Bhairavi./ Savita Uppal.
NR44,3591v	Origin and development of Todi raga./ Gowri Kuppuswamy.
NR44,3592	Sarang ke prakar./J T Shah.
NR44,3593	Raga Malhar./Shanno Khurana.
NR44,3594	Kangra ke prakar./J T Shah.
NR44,4	Five fold classification of music./Indu Raman.
NR44,4	The forgotten forms of Hindustani music./Rabindra Bharali.

NR44,4	Categories of music./Ashok D Ranade.
NR44,4ObR5	Aesthetics of Hindustani musical forms./Thakur Jai Dev Singh.
NR 44, 41 a	Bibliography on dhrupada./ Francoise Delvoyo.
NR44,41	Dhrupad./Indurama Srivastav.
NR44,41ObR5	Aesthetics in dhrupada./Falguni Mitra.
NR44,41Ot2	Dhrupad and khyal form in Indian music./Chetan Karnani.
NR44,41;1a	Dhrupad discography./Nancy Lesh.
NR44,41;14a	Discography of EP-LP recordings of dhrupad music./Peter-F Muller.
NR44,412v	Evolution of khyal./M V Dhond.
NR44,412	Khyal./Bonnie C Wade.
NR44,412Ok6V	The khyal ang of the Vishnupur Gharana./A R Banerjee.
NR44,412:(R5)	Aesthetics laws of khyal./V H Deshpande.
NR44,42v	Evolution of thumri./Sumilk Bose.
NR44,42	Thumri in historical and stylistic perspective./Peter Manuel.
NR44,42ObO	Literary aspects of thumri./C S Pant.
NR44,42Ot552	The Hindustani thumri and its parallel in Karnataka music Javali./S A K Durga.
NR44,42:g(NS)	Dance in thumri./Projesh Bannerji.
NR44,42:1	On thumri taleem./Anita Sen.

NR44,42:(NRY)	Folk elements in thumri./Sushila Pohankar.
NR44,42:(Y)	Sociology of thumri./Vinayak Purohit.
NR44,433	A note on tana./Titte Krishna Iyengar.
NR44,52	Popular music of India.
NR44,52	Light classical music./Poornima Sinha.
NR44,522 v	Musical evolution of the ghazal./ Ashok D Ranade.
NR44,53	Making of the music happen in Qawwali—performance traditions in India./Bonnie C Wade.
NR44,5(Δ25)	Music based on Bhakti poetry.
NR44,5(Δ73)	Sufi music of India and Pakistan./ Regula B Qureshi.
NR44,5(NW)	Down Binaca lane./Raju Bhartan.
NR44,5(Q)	Sacred songs of India./K K Subramaniayam.
NR44,5(Q2)	Bhajan singing style in Hindustani music./Geetha Ravi Kumar.
NR44,6	Indian musical traditions./V H Deshpande.
NR44,6A	Agra Gharana./Panna Lal Mehta.
NR44,6BE	Betia Gharana./Falguni Mitra.
NR44,6G	Gwalior school of music./B L Gupta.
NR441y7K75a	Dikshita; Bibliography./V Raghvan.
NR441y7L67,454	Pancha Patna Kritis of Saint Tyagaraja./Tara Balagopal.

NR441y^7L67,454:g(O) Poetry in the kritis of Tyagaraja./T S Parthasarathy.

NR441y^7L75,454 Sri Muthuswamy Dikshitar—and his kritis./S S Janaki.

NR441y^7M13,16 Compositions of Swati Tirunal./S Venkatasubramania Iyer.

NR441y^7M13,16:(O) Sahitya bhava in Swati Tirunal compositions./V Subrahmaniam.

NR441y^7 M13,16(O31) Note on the Tamil compositions ascribed to Maharaja Swati Tirunal./ S Venkatasubramania Iyer.

NR441 Situating sound and rhythm./T V Kuppuswami.

NR4410bY73(P35) Contribution of Telegus to Karnataka music./T S Parasarthy.

NR4410j5 Influence of western music upon Carnatic music./S A K Durga.

NR441'C Music systems of ancient Tamils./ S Salem Jayalakshmi.

NR441:g Appreciating Carnatic music. Chitravina Ravikiran.

NR441:g Future of Carnatic music concerts./V Sivaswamy.

NR441:g(O) Sahitya in Karnatak music./R Ganesan.

NR441:g(Q133) Ramayana theme in Carnatic music./ S Pasupathy.

NR441,13 Voice culture with special reference to south Indian music./ S A K Durga.

NR441,16	Compositions in south Indian music./ Ranganayaki Ayyangar.
NR441,16(O15)	Sanskrit compositions in Carnatic music./C V Narsimhan.
NR441,16;21a	Musical compositions in audio cassettes./Carnatic music-Vocal./M D Vedavalli.
NR441,183	Facets of notation in south Indian music./Sharda Gopalan.
NR441,2	Sound and sense in Carnatak music./ R R Iyer.
NR441,22	Swara decorations in Carnatic music./ T S Parthasarathy.
NR441,3	Ragas in Carnatic music./S Bhagyalakshmi.
NR441,3Oj433Ot52	Ragam, tanam, pallavi: past, present and future./T S Vedagiri.
NR441,32	Ganakala niyama (Time theory of music)./R Banumathy.
NR441,3242	Variety of upanga ragas of Karnatak music./Bangalore S Mukund.
NR441,36	Modern mela siddhant./T S Parathasarthy.
NR441,36	The scheme of 72 melas in Carnatic music./T L V Iyer.
NR441,45:(R5)	Aesthetics of some Karnataka musical forms./V V Sadgopan.
NR441,452Ot4	Pallavi and kritis of Karnatic music./ Am Catlin.

NR441,4537x	Selects varnams of the present century./Sitamani Sreenivasan.
NR441,454	The kriti form in Karnatic music./ T S Parthasarathy.
NR441,4551	The musical structure of padams./ Ritha Rajan.
NR441,4552	The jawali form in Carnatic music./ Ritha Rajan.
NR441,4554	The tillana and some of its well known composers./ Sulochana Pattabhiraman.
NR4411,1	Musicology in Tamil Nadu. A short survey./Gowry Kuppuswamy.
NR44114,3	The ragas of Tanjore./E Clements.
NR4412,25	Some rare talas in Kerala music./ S Venkitasubramanian.
NR4437,41	Khyal tradition of Rajasthan./ Ranbir Singh.
NR4447,5(Δ73)	Sufyana kalam: The classical music of Kashmir./M Jozef Rachlozyk.
NR44477	Specimen of Assamese music./John Butter.
NR4475:g(R66)	Krishna theme in music of Bengal./ D K Mukherji
NR4475,41	Dhrupad and the music of Bengal./ Subashree Dasgupta.
NR44841	Wing of fire: The music and musicians of Goa./Mario C Fabrel E Sa.
NR44974,41ObQ4	Buddhist dhrupad, carya in Nepal./ Richard Widdess.

NR44Q7,41	Dhrupad in Pakistan./Basra Khalid.
NR(NW)	The technique of film music./ Roger Manvell.
NR(NW44)	Light of the universe: Essays on Hindustani film music./Aziz Ashraf.
NR(0157)	Rabindra sangeet./Vichitra Santidev Ghosh.
NR(0157):(R)	Rabindra sangeet : A study of its course and philosophy./Tarun Sanyal.
NR(Q)	Religious musics./Praveen Patnaik.
NR(Q).44	Devotional music in India./ Ashok D Ranade.
NR(Q1)	Music in the Vedas./ G C White.
NR(Q2)	Key to Hindu music./Chitti Babu Naidu.
NR(Q2)	A treatise on ancient Hindu music./ Arun Bhattcharya.
NR(Q2),21	Hindu musical scale and 22 srutis./K B Deval.
NR(Q2),3	Six principal ragas with a brief views of Hindu music./ S M Tagore.
NR(Q5)	The music of the Jews./A M Rothmuller.
NR(Q7)	Music in Islam./M L Roychoudhury
NR(Q8441)	Sikh musicology./Gurnam Singh.
NR(Q8441)	Sikh sacred music.
NRV:f	Research on instruments./Arvind Parikh.

NRV:(C5:38N28)	The relevance of Prof. C V Raman to the musical instruments./A Ranganathan.
NRV,822.44'N5	Martial music since independence./ Harold Joseph.
NRV1,22Oj3	Musical instruments; their contribution to the development of the concept of svara and raga./ Indrani Chakravarti.
NRV1,41	A survey of presentation of dhrupad style of music through instruments./ Bimalendu Mukherjee.
NRV1.41'C	Ancient musical instruments of China./Vimla Sarma.
NRV1.44'C	Instrumental music in ancient times./ Krishna Bisht.
NRV12	Classification of Indian musical instruments./B C Deva.
NRV26	The forgotten art of Jaltarangam./ A S Ganeshan.
NRV33Ot5v	Pakhawaj and tabla: History, schools and tradition./Aban E Mistry.
NRV33.441	The major traditions of north India tabla drumming./Robert Gottlieb.
NRV33:1	Old and new systems of teaching tabla./Arvind Mulgoankar.
NRV33,2:(A)	A scientific study of tabla sounds./S M Banerjee.
NRV33,6	Table ke gharane vadan shailiyan evam bandishen./Sudarshan Ram.
NRV351v	Evolution of mridangam./B M Sundaram.

NRV36v	Drums of India through the ages./ S Krishnaswami.
NRV36,	The art of drumming./V Murugam.
NRV36,2	Sounds of drums./B S Ramakrishna.
NRV41	Flute./P Sambamoorthy.
NRV41	Bansuri shiksha./C L Srivastav Vijay.
NRV41Ot4	Flutes and trumpets./Venu Sandal.
NRV432	The decline of nagaswara art./K S Mahadevan.
NRV5.445	String instruments of north India./ Sharmistha Sen.
NRV52,16	Bandish on instruments: with special reference to sitar./ Arvind Parikh.
NRV52,2	On detecting the sound of the sitar./ Rory Mc Even.
NRV52,6S	Sania Gharana aur sitar vadan shaili./ Veena Jain.
NRV522	The history of the mandolin./ Geetha Bernett.
NRV53	The swarode: An Indian musical instrument./Ajay Sinha Roy.
NRV5311OaQ:1	Vina in mythology./Usha R Bhise.
NRV533	The emergence of gottuvadyam as a concert instrument./Ravi Kiran.
NRV54	The Voice of sarangi./Joep Bor.
NRV55Oj61	Violin and harmonium./M B Vedavali.
NRV556	Jose and his beloved dilruba./B M Sundaram.

NRV61	Sanvadini (Harmonium)./Jayant Bhalodkar.
NRV61	Harmonium as a solo instrument./ Jnan Ghosh.
NRV61,3	Harmonium and raga music. A critical look./Mohan Nadkarni.
NRV7	Generating instrumental music by the computer./M G Bindulkar.
NRV7.44	Electronic synthesis of Indian musical instruments./G Raj Narayan.
NRV8.44	North and south instrumental music./ S Bhattacharya.
NRV8,42	Thumri on instruments./Arvind Parikh.
NRV822.44'C	Martial musical instruments of ancient India./K V Shakuntala.
NRV83.44	Indian music and orchestra./S N Ratanjankar.
NRV83.44'C	Orchstra and chorus in ancient India./ Swami Prajanananda.
NRV83.441	Concert tradition in south India./ L Annapoorna.
NRV831	Jugalbandi: Fine art or farce.
NRV832.441	The cutcheri paddhati in Carnatic music./S Ramanathan.
NRYz[7]	Essays in Indian ethnomusicology. Ashok D Ranade.
NRY	Ethnomusicology./J Kunst.
NRY44	Ethnomusicology and India./S Bhattacharya.

NRY44	Ethnomusicology: A study of intercultural musicology./S A K Durga.
NRY44	Uncultivated music of India./ Sudhi Bhattacharya.
NRY44:f	Researches in folk performances./ Ashok D Ranade.
NRY44;1	Aspects of folk instruments./ Anil Biswas.
NRY4411	Folk music of Tamil Nadu./ Shyamala Bala Krishna.
NRY4412	Sopana music of Kerala./Deepti Bhalla.
NRY4412,3:g	Analysis of Kerala folk music from raga point./Afzal Mustafa.
NRY4435	Stage music of Maharashtra./ Ashok D Ranade.
NRY4436:351	Folklore of Gujarat./Jagdish Hasu.
NRY4437	Folk music of Rajasthan./U B Mathur.
NRY4437	The living music of Rajasthan./Vijay Verma.
NRY4437	Monograph on Langas./Komal Kothari.
NRY4443	Culture bearers to society: Saga of the folk musical performers of Punjab./ Alka Pande.
NRY44.52:351	Folk songs from Uttar Pradesh./ Laxmi Gnesh Tewari.
NRY4455	Folk music of Madhya Pradesh./ Arun Kumar Sen.

NRY44593	The tribal music of Kinnaur./I E N Chauhan.
NRY446112;1:88	Naga cultural attires and musical instruments./A Laru Ao.
NRY447	Santhal music./Omkar Prasad.
NRY447	Folk music of eastern India./ Sukumar Ray.
NRY4471	The tradition of Odissi music./ Jiwan Pani.
NRY4475	Folk music of Bengal./Sukumar Ray.
NRY4475	Indian folk music. Bhawalya: Ethnomusicological study./Sukhbilas Barma.
NRY44794:351	Mizo songs and folk tales./K Khiangte.
NRY44841,24;1	Folk instruments and folk rhythms of Goa./Antsher Lobo.
013,1:gx1,1:g(NR)	Thoughts on music in Artistotle's politics./Sitansu Ray.
015:gx1,1k	A glossary of Natya Sastra./ Naresh Gupta.
015:gx1,1	Natyasastra./Bharat.
015:gx1,1:g(NRV)	Music and music instrument in Natya Sastra./C Rajendran.
015:gx1,1:g (NT)	Theatre according to Natya Sastra of Bharata./R P Kulkarni.
015:gx1,1,3:g	Study of Abhinava Bharati. (of Abhinav Gupt)./Manjul Gupta.
015:gx8,1	Kavya Prakash of Mammata./ Ganganath Jha.

015:gxE55,2	Bhoja's Srngara Prakash./ V Raghavan.
015:gxH10,3	Gitagovinda./Jayadeva.
O15:g(NR)	Music in Sanskrit literature./V Raghavan.
015,2:g(NR)	Music in Sanskrit drama./G T Deshpande.
0153,1K80:g(NR)	Bulleh Shah. The mystic music./ K S Duggal.
0157,1M61:g(NR)	Tagore's thought on music./ Sitansu Ray.
0164,1GO7: g(NR)	Music and dance in the works of Maulana Jalaluddin Rumi./Ali Asani.
0164,1G53:g(NR)	Amir Khusru and music./S H Askari.
O3OaNR	Sahitya and sangeeta./V. Vamanan.
035:g(NR)	Music literature in Telegu./S R Janakiraman.
Q13:g(NR)	Samveda and sangeeta./P K Pajagopal Aiyar.
R65,8:g(NRY)	Folk music in Mahabharat./ Leela Omchery.
T,8:3(NR)	Experiments in music teaching./V Premkumari.
T:3(NR)	Teaching of music./Gowry Kuppuswamy.
T:3(NR44,6)	Teaching in Hindustani music: A critical analysis./Sarvesh Chandra.
T:3(NR).44	Music education in India./ Lalmani Mishra.

T: (NR)	Music in education./J M Desouza.
T:3(NRV612)	Harmonium and the teaching of Indian music./Dipali Nag.
T2:2(NR)	Music in the school curriculum./ Gowry Kuppuswamy.
T4:3(NR)	Music education in Indian universities: An oveview./Indrani Chakravarti.
V4411:72:g(NR)	Inscriptions on music in Tamil Nadu./ Gowry Kuppuswamy.
X8(NR)	Sounds of profit./Saumitra Banerjee.
Y15(NR)	Women singers./T Sankaran.
Y73 (Q7) OaNR44	Musalman and Indian music./ Acharya Brahaspati.
Y9(NR):42:3	Plight of Indian musicians./ Vimal Patil.
Z2,595 ObNR	Music piracy in India./Rajiv Ohri.
(:f)ObNR	Research methodology for music./ Mohammed Haroon.
(:f)ObNR44	Research methodology for music./ S A K Durga.

Bibliography

Deva, B C Classification of Indian musical instruments. *Journal of the Indian Musicological Society*. January 1976, vol. 4, no 1, p. 33-45.

Dove, Jack Music libraries. vol. I, London; Andre Beutch, 1965. p. 48-49.

Mehta, R C Indian classical music and Gharana tradition. New Delhi; Readworthy Pub., 2008. p. 111-112.

Neelameghan, A Design of scheme for colon classification. *Herald of Library Science* April 1969, vol. 8, Articles no P, Q, R, ZF and ZG. p. 97-110 and 180-182.

Rajan, T N Classification scheme for Indian music literature. *Sangeet Natak*. April 1970, no. 16, p. 73-89.

Raman, Indu. Five fold classification of music. *Sruti*. May 1993, no. 104, pp. 31-36.

Ranade, Ashok D Essays in Indian ethnomusicology. New Delhi; Munshiram Manoharlal, 1998. p. 1-25.

—Perspective on music : Ideas and theories. New Delhi; Promila, 2008. p. 68-86.

Ranganathan, S R Colon Classification. Ed.6 New Delhi; EssEss Pub, 2006. (Reprint).

—Prolegomena to library classification. New Delhi; Ess Ess Pub. 2006 (Reprint).

Varkey, O Classification and preservation of disc records. *Sangeet Natak*. April 1970, no 16, p. 90-96.